AF493284

ATALLAH

The Moor of Venice

ATALLAH

The Moor of Venice

A Verse Play in Three Acts

Written by
VICTOR SASSON

Atallah: The Moor of Venice

Copyright © 2022 Victor Sasson

All rights reserved. No part of this book may be used or reproduced without written permission of the author except for brief quotations in critical articles and reviews.

This play is a work of fiction and a product of the author's imagination. All names, events, characters, places and dialogue are used fictitiously.

First edition

ISBN 979-8-9876978-0-1 (paperback)
ISBN 979-8-9876978-1-8 (e-book)

By Victor Sasson

Novels:
Destined to Die
Confessions of a Sheep for Slaughter
Dr. Bush and Mr. Hide
King Jehoash and the Mystery of the
*   Temple of Solomon Inscription*
The Second Coming
Utopia's Pirates

Plays:
The Marriage of Maggie and Ronnie
Shylock of Venice
King Caliban
Elijah the Tishbite
Atallah, the Moor of Venice

Poetry:
Collected Poems

Non-Fiction:
Essays from Occupied Holy Land
Memoirs of a Baghdad Childhood

Atallah the Moor of Venice is fully protected, worldwide and in whatever form, by the author's copyright. All rights, including professional, amateur, motion picture, radio, television, recitation, public reading, translation into other languages, and any method of reproduction, whether photographic, digital, or by any information storage retrieval system, are strictly reserved.

All enquiries should be addressed to the author, who is the copyright holder, at:

victor7sasson@gmail.com

PREFACE

I read Othello as a youngster and I liked it very much, dazzled by its language - whatever I could understand of it (even though English is not my native tongue, and I did not speak it well at the time). My recent reading, after the lapse of decades, raised serious questions in my mind about the play, having myself written and published several plays. I felt disappointment regarding the artificiality of the characters. Diabolic Iago is utterly unbelievable. Othello is portrayed as a puppet. The characters are definitely not realistic. In the theatre, an audience's imagination can be manipulated and so the viewers can be swept away by the language and the action. Out of the theatre, much would seem lacking credibility. No wonder Bernard Shaw branded the play a melodrama, and I believe he also referred to it as a farce.

How is it possible that a cool-minded General, like Othello, one who can command an army and deal with enemy tactics and trickeries, yet cannot sense the machinations of Iago? How can he be so gullible? On the other hand, it is no secret that great men may have defects in their characters similar to those of ordinary mortals. As regards the plot, it may be suitable for an Italian puppet show, for it is too flimsy for an educated and discerning audience. However, the story is based on an Italian one, which itself must have been inspired by Arabian Nights stories (*Alf Laylah wa-Laylah,* in Arabic) where trivial incidents may lead to dire, disastrous ends. In *Othello*, the trivial incident is the careless loss of a handkerchief.

Shakespeare makes it clear through sundry references in the play that Othello the Moor is Negroid.

But Moors are not Negroid. Whether the term Moor referred to a Moroccan or to a Muslim, it makes no difference, as any of these is generally not Negroid. This conclusion is also supported by Bernard Shaw who, in one of his letters that I chanced to read, states that the Moor like the Prince of Morocco in the *The Merchant of Venice* is not a negro. To Europeans of earlier centuries all swarthy persons may have been considered 'black'. In fact, we do not even have to go back centuries. We see this in E. M. Forster's *A Passage to India*, where Indians are referred to as black, even though a very large segment of the population is swarthy, not Negroid. And, in the Zionist state, Middle Eastern Jews have been derogatively referred to by 'cultured' Polish and East European Jews generally as 'black', and are discriminated against.

In *Othello*, Shakespeare drew a caricature of a 'black' Muslim and turned him into a baptized Christian. But what is the reason for this religious conversion since Venice was a cosmopolitan city-state? It clearly betrays the anxiety of Christians and the shaky tenets of predatory Christianity. This is quite similar to the forced conversion of Shylock, as both Othello and Shylock are 'foreigners'. Hence, also, we see Olivier in his 1965's performance crossing himself numerous times throughout the play so as to convey to his Christian audience that Othello is a truly faithful Christian and not a Muslim or a barbarian. Yet he is portrayed by Shakespeare as an emotional lunatic, gripped with the disease of uncontrollable jealousy. Thus, our author made a religious conversion but retained the character's *supposed* emotional and cultural temperament – that of a volatile North African/Levantine, non-European, with explosive unrestrained behaviour. We see this also when Othello slaps Desdemona in front of the Doge's emissary to Cyprus. Othello behaves like a crazed African native. But all of this conflicts with the nobility and calmness of his portrayed character as a distinguished leader and an army General. Indeed, in Olivier's version, Othello is turned into a hysterical and unpredictable character. This may have been the aim of the playwright himself. But, surely, there is a limit to how low an illustrious soldier can succumb in the face of a perceived personal tragedy.

Now, while in the play Othello relates to Desdemona his military experiences and exploits in war, he says nothing about his childhood days, his upbringing, or his reasons for settling down in Venice. Even more bizarre, Desdemona does not inquire about these personal matters. This is a major fault in the play. What compensates for this fault is the powerful poetic language employed. However, we can claim that we go to the theatre to view a play, not to listen to high and mighty poetic passages, some of which are too lengthy and serve no dramatic purpose.

There are a number of inconsistencies in *Othello*. I shall mention a couple that I myself encountered. In Act Three, scene 3, Iago asks Othello if Cassio knew of his wooing of Desdemona. Othello answers that he knew 'from first to last', which clearly implies that Cassio also knew about the special handkerchief which Othello says was his first token of love given to Desdemona. Yet, when Cassio finds the handkerchief in his quarters, he says the handkerchief must belong to *someone* and would be soon claimed! Then there is this strange and unconvincing coincidence when Bianca appears in the middle of the night at the scene where Cassio has just been injured in a planned attack by Iago!

Regarding the name Othello, hardly any source I have consulted questions the reason for a north African with a German name (Otho=Otto). It is far more natural to associate such a man - a Moor or *Maghrebi*, in Arabic - with the Arabic name Atallah. The term *'atah* means 'gift' and Allah is the name of God in Arabic. Allah is akin to Hebrew El, Eloah, and Elohim and is used in all Arabic speaking countries by Muslims, Jews, and Christians in reference to God. Thus, Atallah would be equivalent to the Hebrew name Nethanel (or Nethaniel) – i.e., Gift of God. Hebrew *Natan* or *Nathan* (give; gift) and El=God (short for *Elohim*, as in for example, *Bethel*=House of God, in English).

The last scene in *Othello* deserves discussion. Othello refers to 'a malignant and turbaned Turk' in Aleppo and how he had stabbed 'the circumcised dog' before he stabbed himself with the same weapon after strangling Desdemona. As a Muslim, the Turk is of course assumed to be circumcised. In the Book of Genesis, circumcision is a holy rite enjoined on all Jews, and was later adopted by Islam. There are very negative references in the Books of Judges and Samuel to *uncircumcised* people, such as the Philistines, and Goliath himself. An uncircumcised person is not a member of the Israelite Covenant, and is assumed to be a pagan - a worshipper of other gods. Therefore, it is quite bizarre that Shakespeare treats circumcision in negative terms in his reference to the Turk, even though he must have known that Jesus, as a Jew, was himself circumcised. Further, the Turk is referred to as a dog, just as Shylock the Jew in *The Merchant of Venice* is called 'a cutthroat dog' by the Christian Antonio. All these elements compel me to revise my opinion voiced in the Preface to my play, *Shylock of*

Venice, in which I said Shakespeare could not have been anti-Jewish. I am now convinced that the author of *Othello, The Merchant of Venice*, as well as *The Tempest* – where the native Caliban is converted to Christianity - is a Christian bigot, thoroughly racist, anti-Muslim, and anti-Semite.

I wrote the first draft of this play during the pandemic scare, specifically between mid-April and mid-June, 2020. Later on, I undertook revisions of the basic draft, giving additional dialogue. The original structure I first envisioned has remained unchanged.

V. S.

June 2021

Dramatis Personae

Duke of Venice

Venetian Senators

Atallah *a General in the Venetian Army*

Cassio *his Lieutenant*

Iago *his Ancient*

Montano *Governor of Cyprus*

Brabantio *father to Desdemona*

Julia *wife to Brabantio*

Desdemona *daughter to Brabantio and, later, wife to Atallah*

Emilia *wife to Iago*

Bianca *Cassio's mistress*

Roderigo *a Venetian gentleman*

Cypriot Officials

Three Cypriot Ladies

A Fool

Officers, Messengers, Attendants, Guards, Sailors, Soldiers, musicians, etc.

ACT ONE

Scene One

A street in Venice, within sight of Brabantio's House.

Enter Iago.

Iago

There is her house! If I could scale it,
Get hold of her and elope, I would do it.
Ah, Desdemona!
How sweet her name sounds on my parched lips!
I must have her or else I must hate her.
My advances she rebuffs with petty,
Feminine wiles, harping on my being married,
Which is true; and says she has found her man -
A prince charming and a noted warrior -
And can think of none other for a husband.
Well, her doting on the Moor unsettles me,
Sealing the matter as to what I should do -
Unless her parents manage to make her see
The error of her judgement.
As to the Moor, what is he but a boor
Dug out from the Sahara, having settled here,
In Venice, after long military service
In sundry foreign lands - a mercenary,

And a mere Mohammedan, a *kafir* –
As they would say in his own barbaric tongue –
One that has no place in our Christian Venice.
He has slighted me by choosing an upstart
As his lieutenant - Cassio by name -
A mere cipher in the arena of war,
And made me an ensign, a standard bearer.
Yet I've seen combat in wars, far and near,
And I know my own worth. But not to worry:
I'll show this general what a field marshal
I am in the art of intrigues and villainy –
To bring him down from his lofty position,
Should he wed Desdemona and defile her
With his foreign seed.
Yes, I'll wage a war of attrition on him.
For though he is rated a great tactician,
I can make a salad of this Saladin.
Here comes one that never tires of courting her.

 Enter Roderigo.

Roderigo
Good day, Iago!

Iago
 And Good Day to you, sir!
Heading to Desdemona's house again?

Roderigo
At her parents' invitation. I am full
Of hope, Iago. Do not dampen my prospects.

Iago
For your perseverance, I commend you,
And wish you full success, but in truth,

You are deluding yourself. My advice:
Seek your happiness elsewhere. Our lady
Has already chosen her one and only.

Roderigo
Who can that be?

Iago
        Our General. The Moor.
He has made a marked conquest without even
Drawing his sword or firing a bullet.

Roderigo
But how can I give up, and her parents
Fully support me in my plight as a suiter.

Iago
It will be a new and brave age when children
Obey their parents in matters of the heart.
Her folks, I assure you, will have little say
In her choice for a husband.

Roderigo
        I am desperate.
I want her so badly, so badly, Iago.

Iago
Scores of Venetian eligible bachelors
Have despaired of winning her. What chance
Have you of success?

Roderigo
        I cannot think
Of anyone else for a wife. It must be
Desdemona or else I'm doomed to perish.

Iago
Perish the thought! You are stricken, I see,
And perforce you must submit your heart
To the agony of unrequited love.

Roderigo
With my financial means, Iago, I can fulfil
All her dreams.

Iago
     If you can buy her love,
Why not? But from what I know of her –
And she is a close friend of my wife – she is
Not one that can be enticed by gold. But
What will you do if she marries the Moor?
Will you hang yourself?

Roderigo
     I know not what I shall do.

Iago
I would marry a baboon before I
Do away with myself. What woman is worth
My life, and they are all fickle? If you haven't
Seen proof of it yet, no doubt you will.
Within a month or two of her marriage,
She will regret it and seek her happiness
Elsewhere. But you will not be a candidate.

Roderigo
Leave me to my plight, man. Fare thee well.

Iago
May you prosper in your pursuit, sir.

Exit Roderigo.

A fool with a pocketful of dreams.
Now who is coming this way?

Enter Desdemona and Emilia.

Well, well, my wife and pretty Desdemona,
Hand in hand, with happy faces that portend
Good tidings. And may I ask what good news
Shines through your pretty faces?

Emilia
We've just come back from visiting the Moor.
Oh, to hear him speak was so enchanting!
He spoke of his childhood in Morocco,
Of visiting Baghdad and swimming in the Tigris.
Told us of his exploits in battles on foreign lands
Before settling in Venice. And mark, Iago,
He is over his head in love with Desdemona.

Iago
But I, too, am over my head in love with her.
And my pleas she dismisses as trifles.

Emilia
Shame on you, Iago! You've got a wife!

Iago
Have I? I'll divorce her and marry Desdemona.

Desdemona
Fat chance you have, Iago.

Iago
How come you dote on him and he is black?

Desdemona
Black? Just a shade dark, which to my eyes
And to other women's eyes more handsome than
Your white skin.

Emilia
    I would vouch for that, husband.

Iago
You, too, Emilia?

Desdemona
Besides, looks are not everything.

Iago
How about age? He is older than you by ten to twelve
years.

Desdemona
What has age to do with love?

Iago
And he being a Mussulman?

Emilia
A gentleman - unlike you!

Iago (*to Desdemona.*)
I admit our Moor is not only a gentleman
But also a renowned General, and he has
My full loyalty. But, come now, you are not
Thinking of wedding him?

Desdemona
>What's that to you, Iago?

Iago
You would wake up in the morning and what
Would you find lying next to you? A snoring raven,
Reciting the Holy Quran, and intoning
La Ilaha illa Llah.

Emilia
What a jealous man you are, husband!
I wake up in the morning and I find
A snoring fox lying next to me, with his hands
Betwixt my legs - yet I do not complain.

Iago
Where would you prefer to have my hands?

Emilia
Between *your* legs.

Iago
Then I must mistake your legs for mine.
You see, Desdemona, what a sharp tongue
Emilia has?

Emilia
>Yours is sharper than mine.

Desdemona
I do agree.

Emilia
Oh, and our General told us a story from the
Arabian Nights.

Desdemona

Alf Laylah wa-Laylah. 1001 nights – interesting tales which the clever Shaharazad narrated to the Sultan in her own special way, so that he would not kill her as he did with his other wives.

Iago

And what's the tall tale he told you?

Emilia

It's called *The Tale of the Three Apples*. It goes like this: a man gave his wife three rare apples to keep in a safe place in her bedroom. As he was walking in the market one day, he spotted a slave with one of those apples. In answer to the man's question, the slave said he was fortunate to sleep with a woman who rewarded him with that apple. The husband, quite incensed, went home, killed his wife, dismembered her body and put everything in a bag which he cast into the river Tigris. Isn't that so, Desdemona?

Desdemona

Yes. But in the end the husband found out that his wife did not betray him, and that the missing apple had been stolen by his son who sold it cheap to the slave.

Iago

Interesting tale that teaches husbands not to entrust anything precious with their wives.

Desdemona

That's not the lesson husbands should learn. Husbands should learn not to rush to conclusions and murder their wives.

Emilia
Exactly.

Iago
But did the man kill himself when he realised he had
committed a blunder?

Emilia
No.

Iago
Then he was not a gentleman.

Desdemona
Would you kill yourself to prove you are a gentleman?

Iago
I wouldn't entrust my wife with anything precious in
the first place. I know she would betray me any time
she has a chance to do so.

Emilia
Isn't he right, Desdemona?

Desdemona
Fie, on both of you! How can you be so callous about
such matters? Anyway, my house is in sight. I'll say
goodbye to you both.

Iago
Fare thee well, good Desdemona! Remember me
In your dreams and blot out the Moor from your memory.
He is fit for the battlefield, but unfit
For your soft, scented, and luxurious bed.

Emilia (*to Desdemona.*)
It's your own life, dear. Make your own decision.
Marry the Moor if you are resolved to do so.

Desdemona (*to Emilia.*)
I am so resolved, Emilia.

Exit Desdemona.

Emilia
Come, husband! You need some tutoring,
Which I will undertake at home.

Iago
   I'll be disciplined.
So be it. My wife is a schoolmistress.

Scene Two
A room in Brabantio's house.

Enter Brabantio, Julia, and Desdemona.

Brabantio
Betrothed? Did you say betrothed?
Betrothed to that Mohammedan?
Have you taken leave of your senses, daughter?
This is nothing but a betrayal of your parents,
And a marriage that would be no marriage.
Come now, will you sell your soul to the devil?
Look, how your mother takes this bad news!

Julia (*sobbing.*)
I wish I never lived to see this day!
Why, is there a dearth of Christian noblemen
In Venice that compels you to choose this man
Who is not of our kind?

Desdemona
What kind are we, mother?

Julia
Look how she answers me!

Brabantio
Come now, daughter, renounce this sham betrothal,
And look elsewhere for a husband. The world
Is full of many an eligible gentleman
Who would prostrate himself to call you 'wife'.

Desdemona
It's my own life. Let me seek my own happiness.

Brabantio
Don't we, your parents, seek your happiness?
It's as dear to us, as to you, daughter.
Let's have no more of this Moor. Annul your
Betrothal. Send him a cordial note
That says it was all a misunderstanding.

Julia
Good advice, dear. Take it!

Brabantio
We have seen engagements collapse, marriages
Dissolved, love faded, romance evaporated,
Within the span of a few weeks or months.

Julia
And what's wrong with Roderigo, and he is
In love with you and has the means to support
A family that you would raise. He may be
A bit of a shorty but he is a gentleman.

Brabantio
Don't dwell on Roderigo's shortcomings, wife.

Julia
I have lived with your father's shortcomings,
All these years. One gets accustomed to them.

Brabantio
And I with yours, Julia; and I am content.
So, no more of this Moor, Desdemona.

Desdemona
I will not succumb to an arranged marriage
For the sake of economic security.
And is the Moor a pauper? He has all the means
To support a family.

Julia
But he's the wrong choice.
He is a soldier, and a soldier's life
Is full of hazards.

Brabantio
And what about Cassio?
He too loves you, and he's a gentleman
Able to support you.

Desdemona
Cassio is a dear friend,
But the Moor is all I can think of - no one else.

Julia
Oh, what a headstrong girl you are!

Desdemona
I will say no more. I am determined
To wed the Moor - come what may.
I will live, with what you call, his shortcomings.

Brabantio
Obdurate, intractable, incurable!
Then we will have no choice but to disown you!

Julia
I should've given birth to a boy I so much craved,
Instead of this headstrong, refractory wench.
Oh, woe, to see this day and witness a rebel
In my own house, under my own roof!
Yes, we will disown you. Go your way and marry
This Moor, who will prove your own doom.

Enter a servant.

Servant
Signor Roderigo is here.

Brabantio
Good. Let him come in. Receive your suitor
With proper respect, Desdemona.

Desdemona
I've never been rude to him, but I repeat:
This man has no room in my affections.

Enter Roderigo.

Brabantio
Welcome, Roderigo! How goes the world?

Roderigo
When the time comes and Desdemona offers me
A smile and approves of my pleas, the world
Would again shine and lighten up my life.

Julia
Come now, daughter! Smile at this wretched man
Who loves you. He will no doubt lose his wits
At your silence and unbecoming frowns.

Desdemona
It's not my fault if he loses his wits.
He knows I have another suitor in mind.

Roderigo
Then let me take my leave. I've lost all hope.

Julia
Nay, stay awhile, Roderigo. Do stay.

Roderigo

Why should I stay, seeing there is no hope
Her mind will change? I'll look for a Moorish wife
Since your daughter is enamoured of her Moor.
Good Day, sir. Good Day, Madam!

Exit Roderigo.

Julia

You've lost him forever, Desdemona.

Desdemona

I hope so, mother. I want the Moor to keep.

Julia

Insubordinate girl!

Brabantio

Here is a suggestion you should wisely heed.
Stay home another week. See, if you can repent
Of your intentions. If not, thereafter you leave us.

Julia

Very well spoken, husband. Take note, wench!
You have one week to shed off this weak thing
Which is eating inside you. Otherwise,
Divorce your parents and marry your Moor.

Desdemona

I need not stay here and poison your sight.
I owe you both so much. I take my leave.

Brabantio
Woe unto him that brings children to this world!
They bewitch us when they are sweet toddlers, but
Cheat us of our sanity when they grow tall.

> *Exeunt* Brabantio and Julia;
> Desdemona separately.

Scene Three
A street not far from Brabantio's house.

> *Enter* Cassio.

Cassio
I wonder where she's now!
She, whose sweet face permeates my whole being.
There is her home! Courage, my heart, courage!
I have her parents' approval, and that's
To my advantage. If I could but win her –
She would be mine to treasure for ever.

> *Enter* Desdemona.

Ah, what luck I have! Desdemona, dear!
Where are you heading to?

Desdemona
To Emilia's house, Cassio.

Cassio
You two are inseparable, it seems.

Desdemona
We complement each other with our characters.

She is worldly, and I am naïve and bookish.
But don't tell me you were heading to my home,
If I can call it home.

Cassio
Yes, indeed I was!
What's the matter? You seem perturbed,
In a murky mood.

Desdemona
Yes, indeed I am, Cassio.
My parents wish to pigeonhole me
Into an arranged marriage.

Cassio
If it's arranged, how can it be a marriage
Worthy of its name? It has to be a marriage
Of true hearts; and we two fit the bill.

Desdemona
Aren't you tired of courting me, Cassio?

Cassio
Never! Never, so long as no one else has
Snatched you away from me.

Desdemona
Oh, Cassio, you know
You have a special place in my heart.
Your friendship means so much to me!
But my affections for a husband lie elsewhere.

Cassio
The Moor?

Desdemona

Yes, Cassio. But tell me: how goes the
Lieutenancy?

Cassio

I am gratified by it
And much beholden to the Moor for this election.
And he is indeed a distinguished general,
Versed in the complexities of war, yet may
Not be so in matters matrimonial.

Desdemona

I'll tutor him, Cassio, once we are married.

Cassio

I know women are so good at tutoring
Post marriage. I have seen proof of it elsewhere.
But the Moor, though he has my full respect
And loyalty, comes from a different climate,
Where other passions may prove foreign both
To your taste and upbringing, and these will no doubt
Show up post marriage, not before, and will soil
The blessedness of a peaceful household.

Desdemona

Don't we all have weaknesses and shortcomings?

Cassio

Yes, indeed. I grant that much, but post marriage
Those weaknesses may prove quite disastrous.
Heed my warning, gentle Desdemona!
My advice is for your benefit and the Moor's.

Desdemona

Marriage is a venture just as a battle is –
None of these is immune to failure.
I am prepared to take the risk, Cassio.
I'll say good bye to you!

Cassio

   Adieu, fair Desdemona.

                              Exeunt separately.

Scene Four

A hall in the Senate.

   Enter Duke, Senators, and Officer.

Duke

Disturbing news it is, Officer. You say
The Turks are preparing to invade Cyprus.
Such news we've had before and oftentimes
Turned out to be rumours aimed to distract us
From state matters.

Officer

   This time, it appears
The news is trustworthy, your Grace.

Duke

Call the messenger who brought this news.

Officer

I've told him to wait outside.

Duke
Bring him in. We will question him.

Exit Officer.

First Senator
These Turks will not cease from harassing us.
We have been masters of the island for over
A century. Cyprus is of strategic value
To Venice and we will not relinquish it,
Even if precious blood must be shed for it.

Enter Officer with Messenger.

Duke
Messenger, through what channels did you get
This piece of unwelcomed information?

Messenger
We have spies and sailors, as you know,
Stationed along various land and sea routes
Whose business is to transmit trustworthy
Intelligence to Venice regarding
Any kind of threat to the state's interests.
These routes stretch from Rhodes to Split to Venice.
It takes days if not a week to reach us.
Considering how far Turkey and Cyprus are,
This news is relayed to you as fast as possible.

Second Senator
Have you any knowledge of the strength
Of forces that would try to storm the island?

Duke
Good question, Senator.

Messenger
   Only an estimate.
It appears they are planning a major onslaught,
Some twenty to thirty galleys. The Governor
Is requesting needed reinforcements.

Duke
Then this is urgent business. We thank you
For this piece of intelligence.

Exit Messenger.

We need to buttress our forces in Cyprus
And must act with the speed this plight demands.
Our valiant, adopted citizen, would be most fitting
For this enterprise.

Second Senator
By which you mean our General Atallah.

Duke
Any objection to his appointment?

Second Senator
Considering this is war with Mohammedans,
How loyal would he be, being one himself?

Duke
His previous experience in other conflicts,
Both on land and sea, all speak volumes
As to his loyalty to the State of Venice.

First Senator
I second his appointment. His being
A Mohammedan can only be an advantage,
As he can divine the machinations
Of the Ottomans better than Christian captains.

Duke
It is settled, then.
Officer, summon our captain Atallah.
Advise him it is urgent state business.
All pursuits in hand he should abandon,
And come to see us here right away.

Officer
A short while ago, I had a glimpse
Of the captain with his lieutenant and ensign,
Conversing with certain dignitaries.
I will deliver your message as soon
As I find him.

Exit Officer.

Second Senator
Atallah has recently married and is now
Encumbered with a wife.

First Senator
    The event has been kept
Under cover as the marriage was accomplished
Against her parents' consent.

Duke
    A wife is a shield
To a warrior accustomed to sudden
Irruptions of war. Do we know who the bride is?

Second Senator
No less a jewel than Desdemona.

Duke
Desdemona, Senator Brabantio's daughter?

First Senator
Not many a Desdemona in Venice.
She is one of a kind – beautiful and alluring -
A wife that can indeed offer a soldier
A home blessed with warmth and loving care.

Duke
No wonder we have seen little of Brabantio,
And the little we have seen of him looked glum
And uncommunicative.

    Enter Atallah, followed by Desdemona, Cassio,
        Iago, Emilia, and Officer.

Duke
Welcome, General!

Atallah
At your command, your Grace!

Duke
The Ottomans have formed a habit of
Rousing us from our sleep and reveries;
From our daily business and mundane pursuits.
News has reached us the Turks are scheming
To launch a massive attack on Cyprus.
Montano, Governor of the island, has relayed
An urgent request for reinforcement aimed
At buttressing the island with more troops

And needed ammunition. Great service
You have done us in the past, fighting
Against Christian enemies. Our present foe
Is Mohammedan. Would you undertake
This mission against an enemy that shares
Your own faith?

Atallah

In matters of war, faith dictates
Partiality for those that suffer an illegal threat.
Venice has been my blessed home and shelter.
I've lived under its laws for more than five years.
In defending Venice, I defend my own home.
My allegiance to the state is as firm
As my allegiance to my faith – *Allahu Akbar!*
This cry of faith teaches us it is Almighty
Who prevails over events, and that power
Belongs to Him - the final arbiter.
If the Ottomans are scheming an invasion
Of Cyprus, my duty as a citizen
And a soldier of Venice is to defend
The commercial and military interests
Of my adopted homeland.

Duke

Aptly spoken, General. You have assured us
Fully of your loyalty to Venice
And its interests. Indeed, we know you
As a man of faith and courage who would
Embrace this mission without hesitation.
Cyprus needs your speedy and urgent presence,
And we must send you there without delay.
Depart tomorrow, if at all possible.

On arrival, examine the island closely -
Its fortifications, defences, and its manpower,
Then render assessments to Montano
And to us. At your departure, we will
Assess the number of galleys to send
After you, and these will depart with due haste.
Let me hear what you have to say.

Atallah

By this assigned mission, I am much honoured,
And can hardly wait to embark on it.
But your Grace must know that quite recently
I took me a wife - Brabantio's daughter.

Duke

Your secret marriage, General, became known
To us only a short while ago.

Atallah

There she is behind me. Will it please your Grace
To question her as to what her wishes are.

Duke

Let me congratulate you on a fine choice
For a wife. Draw near, Desdemona. You've chosen
Wisely - a fine man and a trusted soldier.
Your husband is now summoned for a mission
That takes turbulent sea routes, and a venture
On a distant island that may put his life
In danger. Would you renounce your comforts here
And follow your husband, risking life and limb
On a sea journey that has many uncertainties,
And a destination that may witness a savage war?

Desdemona
Your Grace, I will follow my husband rather than
Stay behind and worry to death for his safety.
My own life I put in the hazard with his life,
Come what may.

Duke
What say you to this, General?

Atallah
Since she is so determined to follow me,
Let her do so, and I ask your Grace to appoint
Emilia, my ensign's wife, as her lady-in-waiting.
Both are already close and loyal friends.

Duke
Let it be so, then. Take leave of your wife
And tarry with us for further discussion
Of this sudden crisis.

Atallah
As you wish, your Grace.

(To Desdemona.)

The Duke demands my presence here.
Emilia will accompany you home.

Desdemona
I shall wait for your return, sir.

Exeunt Desdemona, Iago, Cassio,
Emilia, and Officer.

Scene Five
A bedroom in Atallah's house.

Enter Atallah and Desdemona.

Atallah
Well, Desdemona, it is so gratifying
To know your love for me is so great; but why
Choose to undertake such a voyage?

Desdemona
What! Would you have me stay here and count
The minutes, the hours, the days, and weeks;
Hoping, praying, worrying, crying, despairing,
While you are so far away from my presence
And my embrace? I would rather waste away
Within the span of a few seconds than suffer
Such imprisonment. No, I will follow you
Wherever destiny takes you.

Atallah (*opens his arms and embraces her.*)
Ya Habibti! Ya Nur-Eiyni!

Desdemona
You speak now in the Arabian tongue.
And what do you mean by what you say?

Atallah (*kisses her.*)
My darling; light of my eyes!
My love for you, sweet girl, is no less than yours
In weight and substance. You've brightened my life.
And the honeymoon, which we haven't had,
Following our hurried and clandestine marriage,
Will be spent on the rocking seas.

Desdemona
Let us pray for calm seas and pleasant winds
To steer us towards our destination.

Atallah
Inshallah!
Let's to bed early, for tomorrow
We must rise at dawn and embark on our mission.

Desdemona
Yes, General. Your wife is at your command.

Exeunt Atallah and Desdemona.

ACT TWO

Scene One
Cyprus.
At the castle.

> *Enter* Atallah , Montano; Cassio and Iago
> following close behind.

Montano
Once again welcome to Cyprus. We're happy
You arrived without any major mishap.
Rest assured we will make every effort
Towards your wife's comfort and yours.

Atallah
We thank you, Montano, for your concern
Regarding our stay. We shall soon see
What the Ottomans are scheming.

Montano
Your valued opinion of our defences?

Atallah
Overall, the fortifications look good,
But I will make some suggestions regarding
The troops and their effective deployment.

Montano
By all means.

Atallah
Our senate in Venice has ordered twenty-one
Galleys to be dispatched, which should arrive
At Cyprus any day.

Montano
Most reassuring.

Enter an Officer.

What is it, Officer?

Officer
We've just got word that the Turks, albeit ready
To launch their galleys and head towards Cyprus,
Have changed their plans so as to attend
To a brewing uprising in the Balkans.

Atallah
How reliable is this news?

Montano
I can vouch for its complete veracity.
Our intelligence sources are most reliable.

Atallah
Then this is indeed good news, Montano!
Be that as it may, we will remain vigilant
As to what the clever Turk may devise.

Exit Officer.

Our galley ships are very well fortified
With three or four cannons - a plus compared
With Turkish galleys which carry one or two.
We must acknowledge the fact that Turkey's
Major advantage is their proximity to Cyprus.
While they can get reinforcements within hours
Or a day, we would need a week, at least.
But good news, Montano.

Montano
    If you wish,
We may retire to my quarters, where you
Can consult sundry maps and documents
Regarding previous attempts by the Turks
To take possession of our island.

Atallah
Definitely, Montano. Lead the way.

Montano
I think it proper to celebrate a bit,
And have some sort of a ball at the town hall,
To which some officials would be invited;
And, of course, your wife and whomever you wish
To invite. What say you to this, General?

Atallah
By all means, Governor. Go ahead with it,
So long as Cyprus is well-guarded.

Montano
Good then. We'll fix the day and hour.

Atallah (*to Cassio and Iago.*)
Go about your duties. I'll be conferring with the Governor.

Exit Atallah and Montano.

Iago
So, the Turks are engaged elsewhere.

Cassio
So, it seems. But as our General has said,
We must remain vigilant and stay put here,
Until we are assured the island is not
Under imminent or planned invasion.

Iago
This gives us time to pursue our interests.
And of course there will be a ball as we have
Just now heard Montano say. By the way,
I've noticed you have a new lady friend.

Cassio
Yes. Bianca. A sweet little thing.

Iago
Good for you! Aiming to marry her?

Cassio
I am not sure she is the marrying type,
But she swears she cannot live without me.

Iago

So, she must be good for fun and frolic.

Cassio

Ha, ha! Fun and frolic. Very well put, Iago!
You are lucky. You have a wife to play with.

Iago

You are lucky, too. You have your freedom.
One day it's Bianca, the next day, Francesca.

Cassio

Don't be jealous, Iago. Go, get yourself
A courtesan or a concubine. There are
Many from which to choose, and she would do things
Your wife Emilia wouldn't even contemplate.

Iago

What Emilia can contemplate you have no clue.
But I know you were once fond of Desdemona.
Then you lost her to the Moor.

Cassio

    I am still
Quite fond of her, but what's past is past.
She is now another man's wife. Let's attend
To our duties, shall we?

Iago

    Sure, Lieutenant.

Exeunt separately.

Scene Two

An area outside the castle.

    Enter Bianca and Fool.

Bianca

I am new in this area. Can you tell me where
Lieutenant Cassio's quarters are?

Fool

How would I know who and where Cassio is and the
reason he was quartered?

Bianco

Lieutenant Cassio is second to General Atallah, both
newly arrived in Cyprus to help us fight the Turks.

Fool

Fight the Ottomans? I've heard of a Venetian Moor
arriving in Cyprus. But I am Greek and the whole
thing is Greek to me. How can Venetians fight
the Turks all the way from Venice? I may not be a
philocipher, but the whole thing beats me. You see,
wench, a simple fool like me can discern a bigger one
and the Venetians are bigger fools because sooner or
later the Turks will take over. And I am not against it.
After all, I like their *shish kebab.*

Bianca

Go to, why don't you answer to the point?

Fool

Ever heard a philocipher answer to the point?
Anyway, are you a client of Cassio or is he a client of
yours?

Bianca

Zounds! We are lovers. We dote on each other.

Fool

On each other! Nice to hear. So long as you are not under each other.

Bianca

What a fool you are!

Fool

I acknowledge the compliment, with thanks. But I am an amateur fool; the professionals are in the government.

Bianca

No day passes without meeting a fool.

Fool

The world is full of fools and fools are full of worldly wisdom. And I'm always happy to help a damsel in distress. There are barracks some distance from here. So, walk all the way straight ahead, then turn to your right, turn to the left, and when you reach a farmer's market, you will notice an open space, and nearby are the barracks. But if your lover is a lieutenant, he must have his own private lodging, too.

Bianca

Here is half a ducat for your trouble.

Fool

And here's a piece of advice. Make sure you don't get in trouble with that lieutenant of yours.

Bianca
What kind of trouble?

Fool
Getting pregnant. What else?

Bianca
What a busybody you are!

Fool
Come, how about dancing the *Syrtos* with me?

Bianca
Dance by yourself. I am Venetian, not Greek.

> *Exit* Bianca and Fool, separately.

Scene Three
At the barracks.

> *Enter* Atallah and Iago.

Atallah
These letters contain important information;
my assessment of the current fortifications
and manpower in Cyprus, as well as my
recommendations. Hand them to the pilot at the
harbour. He should guard them well till they reach
our Senate in Venice.

Iago
I will do it right away, sir.

Atallah

Is that Cassio over there, just outside the gate?

Iago

I believe it's him.

Atallah

What woman is that he is conversing with?

Iago

By her looks and dress, if my eyes do not fool me, it's
Bianca, a born Cypriot of Venetian parentage.

Atallah

What business has she near the barracks, and what
business has Cassio with her?

Iago

In truth, I am not sure. I suspect she is a courtesan.

Atallah

A courtesan? What else you know about her?

Iago

I would not ascribe any wrongdoing to Cassio. The
woman is in love with him.

Atallah

I know of your regard for Cassio, but on your way out
tell him to come over to see me here.

Iago
I will do so.

Exit Iago.

Atallah
I do not like what I see. My lieutenant
Should not associate with a courtesan.
By Allah, this is not proper; not proper at all.
It will give our office here a bad name,
The smell of which will, in no time, reach
Venice itself.

    Enter Cassio.

Cassio, what woman was that?

Cassio
Bianca. She follows me everywhere, sir.

Atallah
Ya-Allah, ya-Sattar! May Allah protect us!
Do you realise, man, what bad name she will
Give us and our mission here and, indeed,
Venice itself, when Cyprus and its citizens
See the General's lieutenant consorting
With a courtesan!

Cassio
    I must apologize, sir.

Atallah
Apologies will not do. Get rid of her!

Cassio
Sir, how? Let me have a hint how to do it.

Atallah
Cassio, this is not a military matter.
If she were an enemy target, I would know
How to answer you. But since she is not,
The problem is yours alone to deal with.
Dispose of her in any way you may choose.
She is not to be seen befriending you,
And you are not to encourage her.

Cassio
I will do my best to get rid of her,
But murder will be out of the question.

Atallah
Do your best, then, man. Get rid of her,
Or get a decent wife to sleep with.

> *Exit* Atallah and Cassio, separately.

Scene Four
A room in Iago's house.

> *Enter* Iago, Emilia, and Desdemona *(holding her
> handkerchief.)*

Emilia
You're always welcome to visit, Desdemona.
Make yourself comfortable.

Desdemona

Thank you, Emilia.
It's good to see you both, but where is Marco?

Emilia

He is such a wily cat, fond of hide and seek.
I'll call him. Marco! Marco!

*(The cat appears and goes directly to
Desdemona.)*

Desdemona

What a sweet cat you are, Marco!

(She fondles the cat.)

Emilia

He likes you so much.

Desdemona

A Venetian cat, after all.

(She releases the cat.)

Iago

We love him, don't we, Emilia?

Emilia

We do, even though he plays his pranks on us.

Desdemona
Here in Cyprus, so far away from home,
What would I do without you, Emilia?
You are my best friend.

Iago (*to Emilia.*)
    I wouldn't believe her.
Surely her handkerchief is her best friend.
It's so close to her heart.

Desdemona
    Iago, it has magic.
It's not just another one of your napkins
To wipe your nose with. It is a token
Of love bestowed unto my husband
By his late mother, then passed on to me
As his first token of constancy.

Emilia
What have you to do with handkerchiefs, Iago?

Iago
This one's workmanship fascinates me.
But perhaps it is bewitched and I shouldn't
Even touch it.

Desdemona
    Charmed, not bewitched, Iago.
It belonged to an Egyptian. Within its
Embroideries, it has buried secrets.
It speaks to me and I speak to it.

Iago
What? It speaks in the Arabian tongue,
And you understand it?

Desdemona
It speaks in hieroglyphs.

Iago
And what does it say, Desdemona?

Desdemona
It says one should mind his own business.
It would not speak to anyone else but me.
And, take note, I was warned not to misplace
Or lose it but to safeguard it as the apple
Of my eye.

Emilia
Are you satisfied now, husband?

Iago
Not satisfied; quite baffled.

Emilia
But why?
That handkerchief is a valid contract
That has fast bounded two hearts together.

Iago
I wouldn't hang my happiness on a piece
Of cloth, however charmed and precious.

Emilia
Don't be critical.

Iago
  I am nothing but.

Emilia
You never gave me any such token of love
And loyalty, Iago husband.

Iago
  I never
Wanted you to be bound by any trifle token,
Which could be misplaced, pilfered, lost.
To hang one's own happiness on a handkerchief …

Emilia
Enough, Iago! Our guest is getting tired
Of your moralizing. Her face shows it.

Iago
Don't frown, Desdemona. It doesn't suit.

Emilia
Let's head to the dining room and have tea.

*(Desdemona negligently puts her handkerchief in
her open purse. Unnoticed, it is snatched up by the
cat, which goes and hides under the couch, and later
hides the handkerchief elsewhere.)*

                              Exeunt all.

Scene Five

The grounds of the castle.

Enter Atallah and Iago.

Atallah

You spend more time with him. Come, tell me.
Unlock the store of your memory and disclose
Whatever you know about him.

Iago

Cassio is a good friend and loyal colleague.
To say or impute anything negative
About him would be sinful.

Atallah

Tush, Iago!
Our present mission here is most sacred.
Duty dictates that we show the people
Of Cyprus and our Senate in Venice
Who we are: soldiers without a blemish.
Ka-Ra-mah - that's the word I would use
In my own tongue. What does it signify?
Ka-Ra-mah is honour, nobility, dedication.
All of these and more. We've pledged to protect
The island of Cyprus and its citizens
And must uphold the highest level of integrity.
We cannot have a lieutenant who drinks,
Associates with courtesans, or makes
A fool of himself in public, for his behaviour
Reflects on me, his superior, and indeed,
On Venice itself. Such things should not happen;
No, not under my command.

Iago

I agree, sir.
He is fond of women, being single.
And I recall he once zealously courted
Desdemona before the prize fell to you.

Atallah

He did, did he? By Allah, this is news to me!
Ah, no wonder she has been fond of him.
Did I say fond? No. More than fond.

Iago

And he of her. It is not a secret, General.

Atallah

No, not a secret; not a secret.

Iago

And who knows what goes behind the scenes, sir?
Behind closed doors, in dark alleys and warehouses.
Illicit love is a disease that lurks in darkness,
Breeds its own germs, multiplying by the second,
Feeds on its carnal, famished compulsions.
And, rest assured, I am as concerned about
Our mission here as you are.

Atallah

I believe you.
By Allah, if she proves a whoring wife,
I will get rid of her. Did I spell it out, Iago?

Iago

Perfectly, sir. You are entitled to your rage.
What husband wouldn't be stunned to find his wife -
The love of his life - treacherous, deceptive,
With honeyed tongue, seeming pure, virginal,
Unadulterated, yet false and corrupt?
Only a dull ass of a fellow would put up
With the shame, the stigma, and the agony.

Atallah

If she proves a whoring wife, Iago,
Will you help devise a scheme for her demise?

Iago

Oh, I hope it will not come to that. But
As your ensign, I will do all I can to help.
My brains I will rack to invent a scheme,
And undertake the task as if I am
Embarking on a military mission.
Let me see. What sorts of pursuits
Your wife has?

Atallah

Singing, drawing, and reading.
These days she is deep into *Arabian Nights.*

Iago

Anything else?

Atallah

Oh, she is fond of sea-bathing.
Since we set foot on Cyprus' soil, she has often
Urged me to bathe in the Mediterranean Sea.

Iago
That's it! How about accidental drowning, sir?
It's quite a clean way of disposing off
A faithless, deceptive, lying wench.
Imagine, we three bathing in the sea,
In a secluded area, as befitting
Your station as a General, and your wife,
Having fun, suddenly finds her feet
Pulled down by some sea creature or other,
And her cries for 'Help!' are too late for rescue,
And in seconds all your plights evaporate
As her last breath show up in bubbles,
And her life terminates.

Atallah
     I like it, Iago!
I like it very much. Your plan appeals
To me. Will you help implement it?

Iago
You can count on me, sir.

Atallah
But upon her demise, would our testimony
Ring true? Can we get away with it?

Iago
What fool would suspect you of foul play?
But to allay your fears, I could hire
A so-called witness, who would be busy
Playing his dice while we pursue our task.

Atallah

Ingenious, Iago! You will be my lieutenant.
That position is yours upon successful
Completion of the task.

Iago

    Ah, position!
The world makes so much fuss about position.
But it is the man that makes the position,
Not the position the man. We see many an ass
Flaunting his rank around, while a more worthy
Is denied his worth and forced to do a menial job.
Yet, to be honest, I cannot deny
That I had craved the lieutenancy before.
But I have got used to being an ensign,
And the position amply suits me, sir.
And, sir, any position under your command
Is a credit to the person who holds it.

Atallah

Let me know more of what you see and hear.
Promise me, good Iago.

Iago

    You have my promise, sir.
Both my eyes and ears I will keep open,
Like a spy scouting an enemy's grounds.

Atallah

Go now about your duties. I have some
Pressing military matters to consider.

                               Exit Iago.

Well, well, what a blind fool, I am - the General!
I have noticed, not once, how fond she is of Cassio.
Only blind love can be so blind to what one sees
Before one's own eyes. The fickleness of women
And the stupidity of men and their vanity!
Ya-Allah! It must have been an infatuation
That drew her to profess love to me, a foreigner
And a Mohammedan, albeit commended
For my military service. But of what value
This praise and honour, compared to the malignancy
Of being a stranger in a land that is not
The land of your fathers? Yet, let me think.
Does this Iago have an axe to grind?
After all, I did pass him over for
The lieutenancy which he so much craved.
But, then, he solemnly professes satisfaction
With his present position. Still, I must be
Circumspect and not rush to hasty actions,
From which there could be no safe retreat.

Exit Atallah.

Scene Six
Cyprus Town Hall.
A ball with dignitaries, captains, ladies, etc.
Musicians playing.

Enter Atallah, Desdemona, Montano, Cassio,
Emilia, Iago. Bianca at a distance.

Atallah (*to Desdemona.*)
Where is your cherished handkerchief?

Desdemona
How silly of me to forget it.

Atallah
And you are so fond of fondling it.

Desdemona
I miss it. Truly so, dear.

Atallah (*to Iago.*)
Are my orders regarding the guards carried out?

Iago
To the letter, sir.

Atallah
Good.

Montano
I hope, General, we shall all have some good time
this evening.

Atallah
I hope so, too, Montano. Everything looks fine.

Montano
There are light refreshments as well as liquor to
enjoy.

Atallah
My faith forbids me to touch liquor.

Montano
Oh, yes. I forgot. But surely you will enjoy the food
and delicacies on the table. We are here in between

East and West, and our cuisine has borrowed some
recipes from the surrounding countries.

Atallah
I can smell the aroma of the *shish kebab.*

Desdemona (*to Atallah.*)
Shall we dance, husband?

Atallah
I do not dance.

Desdemona
I can teach you, if you are willing to learn.

Atallah
I will prove a poor pupil.

Montano
May I have the pleasure of dancing with your wife,
then, General? You don't want her to be bored on a
night like this.

Atallah
If she so wishes.

Desdemona
By all means, Governor.

(Desdemona and Montano proceed to dance.)

(Two Ladies approach Atallah.)

First Lady
Oh, General, we have heard great things about you.

Atallah

That's gratifying to hear.

Second Lady

A Moor in the service of Christian Venice! We are so happy you have come to defend our island here. Shame on the Ottomans for wanting to take it away from us.

Atallah

No need to worry, ladies, as long as I am in command.

First Lady

Isn't that reassuring! And what a beautiful wife you have! Such refinement and loveliness!

Second Lady

Absolutely. But tell me, are your womenfolk well treated in your native land?

Atallah

They are treated according to their deserts.

First Lady (*to second lady.*)

Ah, and he is a wit, too, besides being a General!

Atallah

I picked up a few things from living in Venice.

Second Lady

In your old home country do husbands beat up their wives?

Atallah
Only if the wife asks for it.

(Everybody laughs.)

Enter a third lady.

Third Lady
Oh, what a charming wife you have, General! And
she dances like an angel, floating through the air.

Atallah
Thank you, madam.

*(Montano and Desdemona return from
     their dance.)*

Desdemona
Ah, it's so refreshing! You have no idea
What you are missing, my dear husband.

Atallah
What am I missing?

Desdemona
The joy of movement to music.

Atallah
I've seen the Darvish dance his whirling dance,
And I can believe what you say.

Montano
Your wife dances gracefully.

Desdemona
I enjoyed dancing with you, Governor.

Third Lady
Ah, I wanted to ask you, General, what do husbands do in your home country when they discover their wives cheat on them?

Atallah
Most husbands prefer to see their wives' heads off.

(Everybody laughs. Desdemona frowns.)

Third Lady
I wonder what your wife thinks of that.

Desdemona
He is just humouring you. A Mohammedan will not shed innocent blood.

Third Lady
I suppose they must strangle their wives to avoid shedding blood.

First Lady
Come along, ladies! Excuse us, General.

Exit three ladies.

Emilia
Well, Iago, shall we dance?

Iago
I will try with one of those pretty young ladies over there. They seem anxious to dance.

Emilia

Deserter, that's what you are, Iago!

Iago

Since I still have to feed you, you cannot brand me a deserter.

Cassio

I will dance with you, Emilia.

Emilia

That's what I call a lieutenant and a gentleman. Fare thee well, husband!

(Emilia and Cassio proceed to dance.)

Atallah

Is that how you treat your wife?

Iago

You should see how she treats me at home, sir.

Atallah

How does she treat you?

Iago

Like a refractory child to be whipped.
We are ever at each other's neck, fighting,
Arguing, hurling insults at each other;
And yet, we love each other, or pretend
We love each other for the sake of seeming
Harmony.

Atallah

It's a solid marriage then.

Desdemona
Thanks to Emilia, who is a true wife,
And whose company I truly cherish.

> *(Cassio and Emilia come back from their
> short dance.)*

Emilia
Oh, I am exhausted. Your lieutenant has had
More than enough of liquor and his breath
Was all over me; but otherwise he is all fun.

Cassio (*salutes Atallah.*)
Salamu Aleikum, General! May I have
The pleasure of dancing with your wife?

Atallah (*enraged.*)
You are drunk!

Cassio
I had too much to drink, sir. I'll get over it.

Atallah
It will make no difference!

> *(Bianca, dressed fashionably, approaches Cassio
> and the rest.)*

Bianca
Cassio, I've been looking for you all over the place.

Cassio
Bianca! You are here!

Bianca
Yes, I am here. Why are you surprised?

Cassio
Leave us alone for now, Bianca. The General
Is not in good mood.

Bianca
　　All right. I'll be around.

　　(Bianca moves to another area in the hall.)

Atallah
You are no more my lieutenant, Cassio!

Desdemona
He is only a bit intoxicated, dear.

Cassio
To my last breath, I am your lieutenant, General.

Atallah
Not any more, Cassio!

Iago
He will get over this soon, sir.

Atallah
My lieutenant should know the limit
Of his tolerance for alcohol. At all times
He should be sober with his wits about him.
A lieutenant is not an ordinary recruit
And should be a model to those below his rank.

Montano, we will take our leave now, myself
And my wife.

Montano
    As you please, General.

Exeunt all.

ACT THREE

Scene One
A hall in the castle.

Enter Desdemona and Emilia.

Desdemona
I've made a thorough search for it. I did.
Oh, I am so distressed about my negligence!
I get absent-minded at times, Emilia.

Emilia
Don't make yourself sick about it. After all
It's a handkerchief, albeit dear to your heart.

Desdemona
My solemn promise I gave not to lose it.
My lord will be mad when he gets to know
I've lost it. And he's soon bound to find out.

Emilia
You will soon find it, rest assured. We often
Lose things by oversight, only to find them
A moment or two later. Now, let me think:
Remember, you came to visit us recently.
Perchance you lost it in our house.

Desdemona

But I am sure I placed it in my purse,
And I ransacked my purse so many times;
But the handkerchief has vanished.

Emilia

Iago and I will make a thorough search.
If you lost it in our house, we are bound
To find it, and I will bring it back to you.

Desdemona

Oh, I do hope so Emilia, and come back
With it as soon as you find it.

Emilia

   I will, my lady.

                                        Exit Emilia.

Desdemona

My husband's soft manners towards me
Have so much changed. He is irritable
And suspicious, for what reason, I cannot tell.
Yet I feel as though I myself am to blame
For this sudden change. With my unflinching
Love for him, I know I am blameless.
Oh, who's that coming this way? It's Cassio!

   Enter Cassio.

Cassio

I've been trying to see you, Desdemona.

Desdemona

Why look you so out of colour, good Cassio?

Cassio
How should I look, having lost my lieutenancy?
An extra drink or two tipped the balance to
This grievous loss. Oh, Desdemona, will you not
Plead my cause with your husband, and have him
Restore my post? Won't you do this much for me?

Desdemona
Cassio, your loss is felt here in my heart.
It grieves me so much for this degradation.
Rest assured I'll do my best to plead your cause.
But my husband's usual self and his manners
Towards me, his wife, have very much changed;
And I cannot account for the cause.

Cassio
Could the cause be the business of the state?

Desdemona
It must be something closer to home. An irksome
Business of the state would draw him nearer
To the person most intimate with him;
And I, his wife, would be that very person.
But, Cassio, my best I will do to make him
Restore your post

Cassio
    Do so, Desdemona.
Or else, my military career is finished.

Desdemona
Arm yourself with patience, Cassio.

Cassio
I will, my lady.

Exeunt, separately.

Scene Two
At the castle.

Enter Atallah and Montano.

Montano
Yes, the galleys have been spotted by our sailors. We expect them at the harbour this afternoon.

Atallah
Very good. I will speak to the captains at the first opportunity.

Montano
Certainly.

Atallah
We need to discuss with them issues relating to logistics.

Montano
I will notify you as soon as a meeting with the captains is possible.

Atallah
Do so, Governor.

Exit Atallah and Montano.

Scene Three
Iago's House.

Enter Iago and Emilia.

Emilia

Come, Iago, and let's do a thorough search
Of our house. Search this side and I will search
The other side. Leave no stone unturned.

Iago

I will detach each and every brick of our house,
In search of that precious handkerchief.

Emilia

Save your humour for another occasion.
My good lady is distraught at this loss.
You know how jealous her husband is, and how
He might reach false suspicions regarding
The item's disappearance. So, make a thorough search.

Iago

Our Moor's priorities are topsy-turvy.
Granted, it's a precious token, but to hang one's
Happiness on a piece of cloth – that's beyond me!
Yet, rest assured, I will look for the handkerchief
With candle.

Emilia

　　Do so. And do undertake
This task with the seriousness it deserves.

Exit Emilia.

Iago (*searching the premises.*)
And if by chance I find it, I'll use it for
My own dark purposes. Now let's see.
I have an inkling of what happened to it.
Our cat, Marco, is as clever as I am,
And a shrewd manipulator – a copycat.
The handkerchief could have been filched by him,
Having read my mind with his own instincts.
He is clever enough to spot a precious
Article and hide it somewhere, where it would be
Quite hard to find. Or, perhaps he was just
Jealous of the affection its owner showered on it.
Ah, let's see here, which is one of his haunts.
Well, well, *there it is!*
The irreplaceable handkerchief! The one
That will prove to be a life or death to its
Pitiable owner – oh, Desdemona!

> *(He takes the handkerchief and puts it securely in*
> *his pocket.)*

Emilia (*within.*)
I am still searching. Any luck, Iago?

Iago
None so far, dear.

Emilia
Keep looking for it.

Iago
I am doing all I can.
Let me now think. I will plant this thing
In Cassio's quarters. He has seen it before

And knows to whom it belongs. With some luck,
And some charm from the handkerchief, events may
Lead to ends that would with success crown the day.

Exit Iago.

Scene Four
A room in the castle.

Enter Atallah and Desdemona.

Desdemona
I will have a word with you, my lord.
It's about Cassio …

Atallah
　　What's wrong with Cassio?

Desdemona
He is distraught at the loss of his post.
One minor error of judgement, and he is
Fired, subjected to humiliation and shame
Before the eyes of the military and the world.

Atallah
And what's that to *you*?

Desdemona
How come you speak to me like that?

Atallah
How am I to speak to you?

Desdemona
As your loving wife; yet you address me
With contempt in your voice that makes me shudder.

Atallah
Are you my wife, Desdemona? Come, speak up!

Desdemona
A most bizarre and unfair question
From the person I love so much.

Atallah (*yells at her.*)
Liar, liar, liar!

Desdemona
Why liar? Why? What is this outburst
That does not become the head of an army?

Atallah
What is it between Cassio and you?
Come, tell me. Out with it!

Desdemona
But Cassio has always been a cherished friend
To both of us – and a colleague of yours.

Atallah
He is now neither my friend nor my lieutenant;
But I suspect he is a cherished friend of yours.

Desdemona
What are you insinuating, husband?

Atallah

Don't call me husband. Tell me what is going on
between you and Cassio?

Desdemona

He has asked me to plead with you to have his
lieutenancy restored to him.

Atallah

Is that all?

Desdemona

By all that is sacred, that is all.
What makes you think there is more to it?

Atallah

He makes no love to you behind my back?
And you to him? Come, out with it!

Desdemona

What devil has caused you to think such a thought?
And what proof do you have for this grave
And unjust accusation? Come, tell me!

Atallah

My source for this is a most reliable one.

Desdemona

What source can be so evil to report
Such a vile thing to you? What is it; who is it?
Give me a way to defend my honour.

Atallah

Your *honour! What* honour? You are a whore!

Desdemona

I am not! I am your true, faithful wife.
Tell me the source of this vile accusation.

Atallah

I cannot disclose the source. It is most
Reliable, coming from a trusted person.

Desdemona

Then cursed be that source that has thus maligned me!
I am your faithful and devoted wife.
I have loved you and will do so till I die.

> *(She starts crying and takes out a*
> *regular napkin.)*

Atallah

Your fake tears will have no effect on me.
And where is the handkerchief that I've given you
As my first token of love and constancy?

Desdemona

Alas, I have misplaced it somewhere.
We all lose things sometimes, don't we?

Atallah

That handkerchief is *not* a thing. It is
A precious token, and you have negligently
Lost it … Or perhaps given it to your lover?

Desdemona

I have no such lover. Come, name that monster
That has given you that abhorrent notion!

Atallah
Cursed be the day on which I chose to marry
A Venetian slut! I should have stuck to my roots.
Scores of chaste Moorish girls sought my hand
In marriage, but fool that I am, chose you.
Ah, cursed fate that made me set my eyes on you!

Exit Atallah.

Desdemona (*sobbing.*)
Oh, woe is me! What has possessed my husband?
What evil spirit has taken hold of him?

Exit Desdemona.

Scene Five
On the steps of Bianca's house.

Enter Cassio and Bianca.

Bianca
Did you have good time, my love?

Cassio
Yes. How much do I owe you?

Bianca
Shame on you, Cassio! You know I love you.

Cassio
And I love you too.

Bianca
Then marry me. I want you to marry me.
My trade I'll give up and lead a lady's life.

Cassio
We will see about that, Bianca.
Let's give it time. We need more time.

Bianca
I am not a common whore. I am decent,
More decent than many a Venetian wife.

Cassio
When I get my lieutenancy back, and *you*
Change your ways, then we talk about marriage.

Bianca
When shall I see you again?

Cassio
I don't know, Bianca. I must now run to Emilia and
hand her this handkerchief. I know it belongs to
Desdemona but I don't know how it came to be in my
chamber. It's one of a kind.

Bianca
I'll take a look at it.

(She snatches it away.)

Cassio
Give it back to me!

Bianca
Let me hold it for a couple of days, dear.

Cassio
Desdemona must be distraught, knowing she lost it.
She is in the habit of fondling it.

Bianca (*fondling the handkerchief.*)
What's a few days without it? She won't do away
with herself on its account. I want to feel as she does
when she fondles it.

Cassio
All right. But promise to return it to me.

Bianca
I will, my love. I promise.

> *Exeunt* separately.

Scene Six
The grounds of the castle.

> *Enter* Atallah and Iago.

Iago
Sir, I shouldn't have opened my mouth at all.
I regret it. Here and now, I recant
Of whatever I've said. Your marriage is dear
To all who know you. It is your own concern
And no one else should meddle with it.
My apologies!

Atallah
     But what if you are right?
What if you are right?

Iago

What if I am right!
A good question, that is. Have you noticed
Anything suspicious lately? Anything.

Atallah

Ah, she is begging me, down on her knees,
To have Cassio's post restored to him.

Iago

That's it! Why is she so grieved about Cassio's post,
If there is not something behind it all?

Atallah

You are right, Iago. But let's not forget
He has been our friend from the start.

Iago

Of course.

Atallah

Yet you are saying there is something going on
Between him and my wife. What proof is there
For such a damning claim?

Iago

What proof can one
Produce in such a case, except catching the pair
In the carnal act!

Atallah

The carnal act!
What would I do if I were to witness such proof?
Or, shall I say, what would I not do
If I were to witness them in the carnal act?

Iago
I shudder to think what a jack of a husband
Would do, let alone a famed soldier like you.

Atallah
Would I not contemplate murder, Iago?

Iago
What husband would not contemplate murder,
Unless he were a base coward?

Atallah
I would murder her, Iago. Yes, I would.

Iago
Imagine Cassio lying on Desdemona,
With her legs bent to her cheeks, relishing
Each aching thrust that your lieutenant makes,
While she's begging for more with a gaping
Mouth, and your brave lieutenant gratifying
Your wife's famished flesh.

Atallah
    I would slit her throat,
Mangle her body, and turn it into *shish kebab*.

Iago
For while he is lying on her, thrusting his
Tool of lust into her soft, perfumed body,
She lies to you with her sweet, honeyed talk.
Have you not noticed the trickeries of women?
We men are nought but playthings, nay, clay,
In their hands, and they are so adept
At manipulating and fashioning us to
The puppets they so much wish us to be.

Atallah
Yes, yes. Go on, Iago! Go on!

Iago
After all, Desdemona, your wife, is a native of
Venice, whereas you are a Moor and a Mohammedan.

Atallah
That's true, a Mohammedan and I am proud of it.

Iago
And, let's be honest, a foreigner in the eyes of the
world, albeit a distinguished one.

Atallah
That's true, too. A foreigner.

Iago
She is a Venetian woman and Venetian women are famous
for their fickleness. A Moorish wife would stick to you to
the end of life, but a Venetian one … pooh! … I have seen
it with my own eyes when some foreigner sells his soul
to one of our females that has bewitched him. A Venetian
woman would sell her virginity for a pot of pottage, sir.

Atallah
Is that so? What about your wife? Come, tell me.

Iago
My wife?
She is as fickle as a pickle, as any
Of them courtesans. I even heard her once
Saying she would do things under cover
Of night, if not doable under the canopy
Of the sun.

Atallah

Yah-Allah, you take it with such
Equanimity. You show no fuss about it.

Iago

What can I do about it? It's the way of the world. You
marry a wench but you don't know what goes inside
her rotten head. The next day or the next week, she
has had enough of you and wants and needs some
new conquest, or an old one that has been left by the
side. But in your case, sir, as a commander in the
Venetian army, you would be a laughing stock not
being in command your own wife.

Atallah

Ah, why should we men give women rights,
When we are such slaves to their skin-deep beauty!

Iago

Quite aptly put. Yet, since you love your wife
So much, it's best to continue doing so.
That would show the nobility of your soul.

Atallah

Nobility of my soul! You are talking
Of carnal lust contaminating the bed
Of a newly-wed couple; of a husband
And wife, no less. Ah, let me brood a little!
Go about your duties, Iago.

Iago

As you wish, sir.

Exit Iago.

Atallah
If I've been betrayed by this so-called wife,
I will, with Iago's help, undertake her demise.
Revenge! That's the word, and it is so apt
On my lips, and so sweet a thought to my mind.
What method of death will I not contemplate?
Yet accidental drowning while sea-bathing,
Seems to me the best way to dispose of her.

Exit Atallah.

Scene Seven
A room in the castle.

Enter Desdemona and Emilia.

Emilia
What's the matter that you called for me
With such urgency, dear? What is it?

Desdemona
Oh, Emilia, I am not well.

Emilia
    But why?
I've lately been too busy to attend
To your needs, and now I see you look wan
And dejected.

Desdemona
    Ah, Emilia, I want to die.

Emilia

I can't believe my ears, Desdemona.
Why speak of death and you should be full
Of life, happy and contented? What is it?

Desdemona

You are my dearest friend, Emilia. I loathe
To tell you what is nagging at my heart.

Emilia

How can I help if you do not spell out
The cause of your distress, my good lady?

Desdemona

My husband …

Emilia

Yes? Go on! Your husband, what?
Do raise your voice so that I can hear you.

Desdemona

My lord accuses me of being unfaithful.
There, I said it, even though the words
Got stuck in my throat. Oh, my headache!

Emilia

Unfaithful?
How can he make such an accusation?
And you are such a devoted, loyal wife!

Desdemona

He harps on the handkerchief which I lost,
Accusing me of giving it to Cassio,
My supposed, clandestine lover.

Emilia

How can Cassio be your lover, when he has
His Bianca?

Desdemona

It's all beyond me, Emilia.
I cannot account for the abuse I take.
Ah, I wish to die! Let me die!

Emilia

Ah, men and their jealousy! They get more
Jealous than us for the flimsiest reason;
And yet we are accused of being fickle.

Desdemona

I feel near death with grief. Let me lie down
And breathe my last.

*(Desdemona goes and
lies on her bed.)*

Emilia

Where is your husband now?

Desdemona

Early this morning he left to confer
With the Governor, and then with the captains.

Emilia

Then we should expect him back home soon.
Let me get you something to eat or drink.

Desdemona

No, I cannot think of food or drink.
Let me vanish and leave this world.

Emilia

It's your distress that is speaking, not you.
Patience, my lady, and matters will clear up,
Sooner or later.

Desdemona

And it might be too late.

Emilia

Cheer up, my good lady! Cheer up!

Desdemona

Oh, he is so irrational, so snappy
In his speech, and in his behaviour so strange.

Emilia

I hear your husband's footsteps. Keep calm.
I will question him and get the truth out.

Enter Atallah.

Atallah

Well, Emilia, what ails our Desdemona?
If she is sick, call a doctor. They do have
Physicians here in Cyprus, don't they?

Emilia

Sir, my lady has no need for a doctor.
She needs your affection and kind words.

Atallah

When her love is spent on someone else,
How can she expect kind words from me?

Emilia
I am sorry, sir, but I must speak my mind.
The Duke of Venice himself appointed me
Desdemona's personal attendant.
Your wife's well-being is as dear to me
As it should be to you. You accuse her
Of infidelity. Hence, her nagging headache
And her lack of spirit and vitality.
Will you let your wife die of grief on account
Of accusations that are patently false?

Atallah
By what means can you divine my accusations
Are false? Are you privy to her comings and goings?

Emilia
Your wife's character is an open book to me.
Her inner thoughts, interests, and daily pursuits
All point to love and loyalty to her husband.
So, who or what is behind your unfounded claim?

Atallah
You wish to know, Emilia? You wish to know?

Emilia
Your wife has asked me for help, and it is
My official duty to render it as best I can.

Atallah
She is an adulterous wife. That's all I can say.

Emilia
But what proof for this damning claim, sir?

Atallah

What proof can one give in this case?

Emilia

Good men and women have been hanged on mere
Hearsay, wicked report, and unfounded suspicion.
I will not have my lady branded a harlot
On idle gossip. Let me ask who or what is
Behind all this?

Atallah

    I have my source, Emilia.

Emilia

Source? What source? This is sorcery, sir!

Atallah

Call it what you will. She has defiled our bed
With her lust and bewitching looks, and opened
Her heart and legs to her clandestine lover.

Emilia

How can that be true? Death is on her lips.
She would be a singing lark for satisfying
Her flesh - if she were the whore you paint her.

Atallah

She must be feigning illness. I want to see
The handkerchief I had given her as a token
Of love and constancy - a precious token
To safeguard as the apple of her eye.

Emilia
The handkerchief, though it is a precious token,
Has been misplaced somewhere, hidden from us,
But the love and loyalty that your wife
Has for you, still shines. If she were unfaithful,
She would not speak of death. But do let me know
The source of this accusation. It is not
A light matter, and should be well tested.

Atallah (*deliberating.*)
Well tested - you say.

Emilia
How else can one prove anything?
You cannot be judge and jury - not in Venice,
And not here in Cyprus, to which you've come
to defend.

Atallah
You would be shocked to hear my source.

Emilia
Nothing can shock me more than
What you have just relayed to me.

Atallah
Your husband.

Emilia
My husband? What about him?

Atallah
He is my source, and mine own suspicions
That confirm his damning information.

Emilia

Iago?

Atallah

Yes, Iago, your husband. A trustworthy man.

Emilia (*mimicking.*)

My husband, Iago, a trustworthy man.

Atallah

Yes, him, Iago - a good soldier and a trusted colleague.

Emilia

Ha! Ha! Ha! The devil! My fiendish devil!
He whom you passed over for the promotion
That he had so much craved, so much dreamt of?

Atallah

What are you saying, woman? Is his aim
Revenge for passing him over for the lieutenancy?

Emilia

Unless I can find another reason for his motives.
And maybe also for your being a foreigner,
And a Mohammedan, too - in his sight.
And you may not know that he had an eye
On Desdemona before you married her,
Even though we two were already married.

Atallah

I'll cut off his head if what you say is true.
I'll mangle his arms and legs - fiend that he is!

Emilia
You will find no objection on my part.

Atallah
You say that much about Iago, Emilia?

Emilia
By Allah, as you would say, yes indeed!
I do say that much, and more! May the devil
Seize him and off to hell, where he belongs.
I am so outraged. Oh, heaven protects us
From evildoers and their machinations!

Atallah
Let me think. Let me consider how to proceed.
Being an urgent and knotty matter, it needs
And deserves careful planning and execution.
Here is what I would like you to do, Emilia.
To your husband say nothing about what has
Transpired between us today. Come, promise!

Emilia
I promise! My lips I will seal shut until
I hear from you further. Discretion will be
My guidance, with no show of anger.
But he is no more a husband of mine.

Atallah (*agitated.*)
We need to test him and his motives for what
He has relayed to me. I will devise a plan
And will advise you soon of its nature.
Meanwhile, do attend to her needs.

Exit Atallah.

Emilia
Oh, I am so relieved, Desdemona!
Did you hear what your husband has just said?

Desdemona
Yes, every word. Ah, let me have a cup of tea.

Emilia
Will be ready in no time, my lady. Your plight
Will soon vanish, and all matters will be set right.

Exeunt all.

Scene Eight
A hall in the castle.
Guards at the entrance to the hall.

Enter Montano, Atallah, Cassio, Iago, Emilia,
Desdemona; state officials, armed guards and
attendants.

Montano (*addressing the assembly.*)
This extraordinary meeting is at the request
Of our esteemed General who seeks answers
To a very important personal matter.
Under penalty of perjury, anyone questioned
Must speak the truth. General, proceed!

Atallah
My thanks to the Governor for convening
This assembly. The matter is indeed personal,
But it reflects also on the well-being
Of my military staff. Hence, I deemed
The Governor's attendance and your presence

Highly important. I now call on Cassio
To step forward.

(Cassio steps forward.)

Cassio
At your service, General!

Atallah
Cassio, a certain item of love and loyalty,
Bestowed by me on my then fiancé - now my wife –
Has been misplaced. My ensign, Iago here,
Affirms my wife has given it to you -
As her lover - and that you're in possession of it.

(Hushed conversations by some present.)

Cassio
What?
Dumbfounded I am to hear this claim, sir.
The accusation is completely false;
A vile lie and Iago must know it as such.
Your wife, Desdemona, never gave me
The handkerchief you allude to. The fact is,
I found it in my quarters and much wondered
How such an article, so dear to your wife,
Could end up there.

Atallah
I see. In your absence
Who else has access to your quarters?

Cassio
I can think of no one else but Iago.
We two often conferred regarding sundry

Military matters, but since the day I lost
My lieutenancy, we have rarely consulted
Each other on any matter.

Atallah
Step forward, Iago.

Iago
Yes, sir.

Atallah
Were you in possession of the handkerchief?
And if so, how did you get hold of it?
My wife says she lost it somewhere. But where?

Iago
At my house, sir. She paid my wife a visit,
And it was there she lost it. Our cat, Marco,
Must have pilfered it and hid it in one
Of his usual haunts, where I found it.

Emilia (*to Montano.*)
My lord, I cannot hold my peace any longer.

Montano
What's the matter?

Atallah
What is it, Emilia? Speak up!

Emilia
Iago, my husband here, clearly lied to me.
Both of us searched for the handkerchief,
And he was emphatic he did not find it.

Iago

Keep quiet, woman! The matter doesn't concern you.

Atallah

Is this true, or you deny what your wife has just said?

Iago

I meant to give the handkerchief to Cassio,
Whom I knew doted on your wife, and he
Would have handed it to her. After all,
He had courted her before you married her.

Atallah

Your duty should have dictated giving it
To Emilia who is her lady-in-waiting,
And she would have handed it to my wife.
But, with evil intent, you chose not to do so.

Iago

I acted in good faith, sir, according to what
I believed was right.

Atallah

    You lie! And it is a big lie.

Emilia

Oh, what a crooked man you are, Iago!
I am ashamed of you.

Iago

    Shame on *you*
For maligning your husband in public!
Seal up your lips, woman!

Emilia

    I will not.
You have been feeding our brave General
With poisonous lies aimed to ruin his marriage,
By harping on his wife's infidelity -
And she is so pure and innocent.

Iago

She is dross parading as gold, and her husband
Sought to know the ugly facts about her.

Atallah

So, Cassio, what has become of the handkerchief?

Cassio

I meant at once to take it to Emilia
Who would then have handed it back to your wife,
But …

Atallah

But what? Go ahead, Cassio!

Cassio

It was snatched from my hand by Bianca
Who craved to have it for a few days,
So as to enjoy the feel of it. She admires
Your wife so much.

Atallah

    Where is Bianca now?

Cassio

She knew of this meeting and followed me here,
Waiting at the entrance, all ears I am sure
To these proceedings.

Montano (*to an attendant.*)
Fetch Bianca. We'll hear her evidence.

> (*Bianca, dressed in subdued, traditional
> fashion, enters the hall; goes and stands next
> to Cassio.*)

You've heard what has transpired in this assembly.

Bianca
Yes, I have, sir.

Atallah
Will you authenticate Cassio's testimony?

Montano
You must speak the truth, Bianca.

Bianca (*to Atallah.*)
I vouch what Cassio has said is the truth.
And this is the enchanted handkerchief, sir.
Being a great admirer of your wife,
I would not wish any harm come to her.

> (*Bianca goes over to Desdemona, bows, and
> hands her the handkerchief, then returns to
> join Cassio.*)

Desdemona
Thank you, Bianca. You have a heart of gold.

Atallah
Governor, I will challenge Iago to a dual.
He is as good a swordsman as any soldier.

Montano
Proceed, General. The floor is yours.

*(Desdemona draws back to Emilia in fright and
    mutters 'No!')*

Atallah
Iago, get yourself a sword!

Iago
Any sword will do.

Montano
An attendant to give swords to both men.

*(An attendant brings swords to both Iago
    and Atallah.)*

Iago
Here I come, Mohammedan!

Atallah
Viper, I came to Cyprus to fight the Ottomans,
But found an enemy under my own roof,
Conspiring, fabricating, and plotting
Against my own household, for no reasons but
Devious jealousy and base revenge.

*(They start fighting with their swords. Atallah is
    bruised. A general cry of dismay.)*

Just a little bruise. Nothing to worry about.

Montano
An attendant to dress the General's wound.

*(An attendant comes forward with a napkin but
     Desdemona takes it and rushes in to dress her
     husband's wound.)*

Atallah
Thank you, wife.

Desdemona
     My heart flutters. Be careful, my love!

(She retreats and joins Emilia.)

Atallah (*in a hushed voice to Iago.*)
And did you think you could dupe me
Into committing murder? *(louder.)* Oh, what a snake
You are, Iago!

Iago
     I told you what I knew.
It was up to you to believe it or not.

Atallah (*stares at Iago and mutters.*)
Ya Kalb! Uncircumcised dog!

     (Loudly, to Iago.)

Villain, I will not kill you. I will let you live
So that you will curse the day you were born.

Iago
Infidel, I spit on you!

> *(They resume fighting. Iago is injured, bleeding;*
> *he drops the sword.)*

Montano (*to an attendant.*)
Dress his wound to halt his bleeding.

> *(An attendant gets a napkin and dresses Iago's*
> *wound. Atallah joins Desdemona.)*

> *(To guards.)*

Guards, put him in chains, and off to prison.
His punishment will be tailored to fit his crimes.

Cassio (*to Atallah.*)
Sir, I have a brief statement to make.

Atallah
What is it, Cassio?

Cassio
> I am engaged to marry Bianca here.

> *(Bianca draws closer to Cassio.)*

Atallah
Really? Are you both penitent and reformed?

Cassio
We are, sir. And we are very much in love.

Atallah
What can one say against love and lovers?

Montano
I deem it right that we all congratulate
This happy couple for their engagement.

   (A general applause follows.)

Cassio (*to Atallah.*)
I've indeed undertaken to renounce
That thief, named liquor, and turn Nazirite.

Bianca
And I've given up the title of courtesan
And will turn a respectable housewife.

   (Another general applause follows.)

Cassio
May I then beg to have my lieutenancy
Restored back to me, sir?

Atallah
   On condition
You keep your solemn vow, and Bianca nurses
A baby and minds the kitchen, the lieutenancy
Is yours as a wedding gift. When is the wedding?

Cassio
Some two weeks from today, sir.

Montano (*to Atallah.*)
It would be most fitting, General,
To have a ball in celebration of the event.

Atallah (*hugging Desdemona and planting a kiss on
    her cheek.*)
By all means, Governor. I leave it to you
To make whatever needed preparations.

Desdemona
For such an occasion, husband, I must teach you
How to dance, even if it is to the tunes
Of cannons.

Atallah
    Since you insist, I am willing
To learn. Meanwhile, I will look for a new ensign.

Emilia
And I will look for a new husband.

Desdemona
Let's make sure those are two separate persons -
And truly honest and honourable ones.

Emilia
As to Marco, our wily cat, he will get
A good beating from me when I get home.

Desdemona
For heaven's sake, don't do that, Emilia!
Give him a hug for me till I see him again.
After all, he has saved my life.

Emilia

    As you wish.
As to the precious handkerchief, I suggest,
With my help, we frame it and hang it on a wall;
And you take it out to fondle it whenever
The spirit prompts you to do so.

Desdemona

An excellent idea, Emilia. Once you do that,
There will be little chance of losing it.

Atallah

Come, Desdemona. Let's go home and enjoy
Our connubial bliss, without fear of that demon
Who had plotted to wreck ruin on our lives.

Montano

A full report of what has transpired here
Will be prepared and dispatched to the Senate
In Venice.

Atallah

    By all means, Governor.

Montano

Best wishes to our General here and his wife!
Let us retire and enjoy our peace of mind,
With happy, smiling faces, and rejoicing hearts.

    (The sound of sweet music playing.)

(Exeunt all.)

The End

www.ingramcontent.com/pod-product-compliance
Lightning Source LLC
Chambersburg PA
CBHW020601160726
47991CB00002B/823